FOURTEENERS
COLORADO'S HIGHEST
A PHOTO JOURNEY

Roger Edrinn
Photographs, Text and Map

Above
The Timber
Buena Vista, Colorado

MOUNT OF THE HOLY CROSS
A collection of small pools encourage the water-loving marsh marigold
and reflect the namesake formation of Mount of the Holy Cross.

HURON PEAK
Harrison Flat in the Collegiate Peaks Wilderness is home to a group of grassy tarns which mirror Huron Peak.

To improve the overall presentation, the text has been reset into a more open font, the photographs remain unchanged.

Serendipitously, as I was working on this reprint, I got a puppy from the local Humane Society, the first dog I've had since Diente. His name is Piñon and he's a Husky–Collie mix. Just like with Diente,

FOREWORD

I'm discovering the joys and trials of raising a free-spirited critter . . . wish me luck. Perhaps Piñon will appear on future pages of this book or other projects.

Fourteeners–A Photo Journey is still dedicated to Diente, Colorado's only Grand

Slam dog, whose enthusiasm for the mountains encouraged me to climb the Fourteeners a second and third time. Those climbs provided many of the photographs in this book. Enjoy!

Roger Edrinn

Above – Roger and Diente enjoy a sun-drenched summer morning on the summit of Blanca Peak, while the summit of Little Bear Peak is shrouded by a low lying cloud.
Front Cover – Capitol Peak is set ablaze at sunset.
Title Page – Colorado's highest summits, Mounts Elbert and Massive, rise above the foggy Arkansas River valley.

Page 5 – Diente stands next to the U.S.G.S. summit marker on Sunlight Peak, while in the background are the shadowed summits of Arrow and Vestal Peaks in the Grenadier Range.
Back Cover – The rising sun kisses the summits of the Crestone ridge showing: Humboldt Peak, Crestone Needle, Crestone Peak, Baldy Peak, and Kit Carson Mountain.

Published by: Above the Timber
P.O. Box 3179
Buena Vista, CO 81211
International Standard Book Numbers:
Standard Edition: 1-881059-85-5
w/CD-ROM: 1-881059-83-9

LONGS PEAK

The soft glow of sunrise illuminates the Diamond, the vertical 2000-foot northeast face of Longs Peak, 14,255 feet. This solid rock face is a favorite among technical rock climbers. For those looking for a less intimidating route, the trail branches at the saddle, at the lower-right of the photo, to almost completely encircle the summit.

MOUNT EVANS
A rocky outcropping gathers sunset light north of Summit Lake. Although taken in mid-July, the lake still has an icy reminder of the long, cold winter at its elevation of 12,830 feet. Meanwhile, the last vestiges of a July thunderstorm break apart across the rugged summit of Mount Evans, 14,264 feet.

MOUNT BIERSTADT

Late in fall, the grasses turn golden around a rocky tarn and across the windswept upper slopes of Mount Bierstadt, 14,060 feet. Located in the Mount Evans Wilderness, the tarn is is easily accessed from Guanella Pass. Easy, that is, if you don't mind wet feet traversing the willow bogs of Scott Gomer Creek.

GRAYS PEAK • TORREYS PEAK

Not far from this spot a scenic railroad wound its way up the north slopes of McClellan Mountain. The railroad carried passengers from Denver to this overview of Grays and Torreys Peaks. Grays, 14,270 feet, and Torreys, 14,267 feet, Peaks are among the easiest Fourteeners to climb.

TORREYS PEAK · GRAYS PEAK

High on a rocky ridge of Collier Mountain, the late evening sun casts a warm glow. Across the valley in deep shadow is Chihuahua Gulch, a favorite access route for climbing Grays and Torreys from the west. Grays, 14,270 feet, and Torreys, 14,267 feet, Peaks are respectively the two highest points on the Continental Divide in America.

PIKES PEAK

This arch is at the base of the Siamese Twins formation in the Gardens of the Gods Park in Colorado Springs. Framed in the arch is Pikes Peak, 14,110 feet. No Colorado Fourteener has more ways to its summit than the famous Pikes Peak. The Pikes Peak Highway, the Pikes Peak Cog Railway, and the Barr Trail are respectively responsible for the most visitors to the summit.

QUANDARY PEAK

Shrubby cinquefoil, commonly known as potentilla, is never so vivid as
in its native high altitude habitat. Defined against the blue sky is the
sweeping east slope of Quandary Peak, 14,265 feet. Quandary is an
easy climb, particularly in such pristine summer conditions.

MOUNT DEMOCRAT

One of the better Fourteener hiking trails leads north of Mount
Cameron to Mount Lincoln. Note several hikers coming from Mount
Democrat, 14,148 feet. On the skyline, just left of Democrat's
summit is the permanent snowfield of Mount Massive and further left is
Mount Elbert, Colorado's highest.

MOUNT BROSS • MOUNT LINCOLN

The rising sun casts long shadows across the waving grasses of an
alpine tarn, while the higher slopes of Mount Bross, 14,172 feet, and
Mount Lincoln, 14,286 feet, are fully illuminated. Bross and Lincoln
had heavy mining activity and hence many roads and structures exist
to this day. Careful inspection of this photo should reveal some roads,
perhaps a tattered building as well.

MOUNT SHERMAN

Blue columbine, Colorado's state flower, grows in profusion on the south slopes of Mount Dyer. Across Iowa Gulch the abandoned Sherman Mine is visible at the base of Mount Sherman, 14,036 feet. The Sherman Mine ore body is actually several miles east and a multi-mile tunnel network carried the ore to this west side access.

CULEBRA PEAK

Violet sky pilot add color to the high, rocky south slopes of Culebra Peak, 14,047 feet. The elevation here is almost 14,000 feet and still there is a profusion of wildflowers scattered in groups among the barren rocks. Culebra Peak is the highest summit in the Culebra Range, itself considered a subset of the Sangre de Cristo Range which stretches from Salida, Colorado to Sante Fe, New Mexico.

HUMBOLDT PEAK • CRESTONE NEEDLE • CRESTONE PEAK
The rugged Crestone group in the Sangre de Cristo Range contains the last Fourteener to be officially climbed in Colorado. Crestone Needle, 14,197 feet, was first climbed July 24, 1916, by Albert R. Ellingwood and Eleanor Davis. Ellingwood's name graces many Colorado mountain features.

KIT CARSON MOUNTAIN • CRESTONE PEAK • CRESTONE NEEDLE

The soft forms of America's highest sand dunes contrast with the rugged Crestone group. Kit Carson Mountain, 14,165 feet, Crestone Peak, 14,294 feet, and Crestone Needle, 14,197 feet, are the names man has given to these mountains. The left most projection is Challenger Point, a fourteen-thousand-foot sub-summit of Kit Carson, named to honor the memory of the space shuttle Challenger astronauts.

CRESTONE NEEDLE • CRESTONE PEAK

From the summit of Humboldt Peak, 14,064 feet, Diente intently peers into the abyss of North Colony Creek. His viewing technique was always the same—go to the very edge of a cliff and get his head as far over the edge as his meager counterweight would allow.

LITTLE BEAR PEAK

The summit of Blanca Peak is Diente's perch for viewing the goings on below. Frequently his ears would "fly" from mountain updrafts, just like Dumbo. The forbidding Little Bear—Blanca ridge stretches between these two summits. Lake Como can be seen in the trees on the far right.

ELLINGWOOD POINT • BLANCA PEAK • LITTLE BEAR PEAK
A grassy pool in the San Luis Valley reflects a western view of the Sierra Blanca at sunset. Identifiable are Twin Peaks, 13,580 feet; Ellingwood Point, 14,042 feet; Blanca Peak, 14,345 feet; and Little Bear Peak, 14,037 feet.

MOUNT LINDSEY

The Sierra Blanca massif is mirrored on the surface of Mountain Home
Reservoir. Blanca is Spanish for white and Sierra means mountains,
so the Spanish name is very appropriate. Mount Lindsey, 14,042 feet,
is the eastern white mountain in this group. The summits of Little Bear
and Blanca are hidden in this picturesque wave cloud.

MOUNT ELBERT

Early morning fog obscures the Arkansas River valley, while on the
opposite side, Colorado's highest mountain stands serene.   Mount
Elbert, 14,433 feet, is most frequently climbed by either of the two
ridges left or right of the prominent center cirque. The left ridge is
accessed via CO 82, whereas the right ridge uses the Halfmoon Creek
Road.

MOUNT MASSIVE

This north-south string of multiple fourteen-thousand-foot points are what gives Mount Massive, 14,421 feet, its name. This view is typical of what one sees from the Leadville area. When viewed from the south near Granite, the mountain takes on a more humble persona.

MOUNT OF THE HOLY CROSS

The high, rocky ridges of Notch Mountain create a sun-trap to nurture a lovely clutch of sky pilot. Mount of the Holy Cross, 14,005 feet, rises across the valley of East Cross Creek.

Huron Peak

A high-altitude summer morning provides a view up the Lake Fork of Clear Creek. Visible are Huron Peak, 14,005 feet, Browns Peak, 13,523 feet, and Middle Mountain, 13,060 feet. Just out of view, further up the Lake Fork is Cloyses Lake.

LA PLATA PEAK

A stationary cloud reflects the last rays of light onto the snow-draped summit of La Plata Peak, 14,336 feet. Much of the La Plata climbing route is in view, particularly that section from timberline to the summit.

MOUNT ANTERO

The upper bowl of Baldwin Gulch, with one of its small lakes, is off to the left, while Mount Antero, 14,269 feet, basks in the reflected glow of a summer sunset. Hikers most frequently use the road, visible on the west side of Antero, and finish along the south ridge. The south side of Mount Princeton can be seen on the left skyline.

MOUNT OXFORD • MOUNT BELFORD • MISSOURI MOUNTAIN

A collection of stacked stones and weathered boards is all that remains of a structure that was once part of the Columbine Mine. Across Clear Creek, three east–west Fourteeners gather the last rays of a summer sunset.

MOUNT OXFORD • MOUNT BELFORD • MISSOURI MOUNTAIN

About a mile further west, compared to the previous photo, the same three fourteeners bask in the sunset of another day. Mount Oxford, 14,153 feet, Mount Belford, 14,197 feet, and Missouri Mountain, 14,067 feet, are most commonly climbed from Missouri Gulch, partially obscured by the foreground rocks.

MOUNT HARVARD

Just north of Browns Pass on the west side of the Continental Divide,
the view to the northeast reveals Mount Harvard, which is on the east
side of the divide. The divide is the low jagged ridge below and right of
the summit of Mount Harvard, 14,420 feet. Just across the divide is
Horn Fork Basin, the most popular climbing approach for Harvard and
Columbia.

MOUNT COLUMBIA

The waning days of summer see an early snowfall and the green willows take on a subtle golden hue. Reflected on this Frenchman Creek beaver pond is the north face of Mount Columbia, 14,073 feet. The rugged ridge on the right skyline connects to Mount Harvard and is the reason most climbers descend to this gentle valley.

MOUNT PRINCETON

The brilliant winter moon sets in the morning sky while the rising sun casts a warm alpenglow over the frigid surface of Mount Princeton, 14,197 feet. Most hikers follow a road below the left summit and then crossover to the main basin at timberline. From timberline an old miners trail continues in a long arc around the basin to just below the saddle, from there its a steep rocky scramble to the summit.

MOUNT YALE

Strong winds tear clouds of snow off the summit ridges of the Sawatch Range. Here Mount Yale, 14,196 feet, is awakened from a winter sleep by the soft pink blush of sunrise.

MOUNT SHAVANO • MOUNT TABEGUACHE

A carpet of bistort on the flats west of Mount White provide a gentle foreground for Tabeguache's rugged north face. Mount Shavano and Mount Tabeguache are seldom climbed from the north owing to the difficult access. This in spite of the fact that the actual climbs are easier from this side.

MOUNT TABEGUACHE • MOUNT SHAVANO

A midsummer sunset peeks under the cloud deck to highlight the summits of Mount Tabeguache, 14,155 feet and Mount Shavano, 14,229 feet. Jennings Creek is just left of the sunlit ridge.

CASTLE PEAK

A snow- and flower-fringed alpine pond calms briefly to reflect the rugged summit ridge of Castle Peak, 14,265 feet. At the far right, portions of the Montezuma Basin 4WD road are visible and above its ridge is the crest of Cathedral Peak.

PYRAMID PEAK
A field of marsh marigolds high in Minnehaha Gulch soaks up the intense alpine sunshine, while across the valley of West Maroon Creek is Pyramid Peak, 14,018 feet, one of Colorado's steepest summits.

MAROON BELLS

Perhaps the most photographed mountains in America, the popular Maroon Bells recreation area is closed to private automobiles most of the summer. A public bus is available in downtown Aspen for daytime sightseeing. These two photos of the Maroon Bells were taken less than two weeks apart, a testament to the variability of Colorado's mountain weather.

MAROON BELLS

While popularly called the Maroon Bells they are more properly called Maroon Peak and North Maroon Peak. Both are difficult climbs owing to the complicated routes and the maroon formation shale, which is often slippery and always brittle. This perspective causes North Maroon Peak, 14,014 feet, on the right to appear higher than Maroon Peak, 14,156 feet.

SNOWMASS MOUNTAIN • CAPITOL PEAK

The mile-wide, snow-covered east face of Snowmass is the source of its descriptive name. Here seen from Buckskin Pass, 12,462 feet, Snowmass Mountain is commonly climbed via this snowfield. The route takes you to the saddle between Hagerman Peak, 13,841 feet and Snowmass Mountain, 14,092 feet, then it follows the connecting ridge to the summit. Visible to the right is Capitol Peak, 14,130 feet.

SNOWMASS MOUNTAIN
The Pierre Lakes are among the highest and most desolate in Colorado. Seen here from a connecting ridge between Capitol and Clark Peaks, the lakes display their rugged beauty. Snowmass Mountain rises from the south end of the basin and on the far left the Maroon Bells are visible.

MOUNT SNEFFELS

The East Dallas Creek valley is full of gorgeous groves of golden aspen and red gambel oak. These colors play against the rugged summits of the Sneffels Range. Its highest summit and only Fourteener is Mount Sneffels, 14,150 feet.

CAPITOL PEAK

Capitol Creek flows north from its namesake through golden groves of quaking aspen and occasional groups of red oak. At the end of the valley, Mount Daly, 13,100 feet and Capitol Peak, 14,130 feet, dominate the azure late-afternoon skyline.

SAN LUIS PEAK

Lemon- and red-orange-colored paintbrush mingle in a grove of timberline willows on the Continental Divide. Across the divide the soft volcanic form of San Luis Peak, 14,014 feet, merges with late-afternoon clouds.

UNCOMPAHGRE PEAK

High on the south ridge of Wetterhorn Peak, rosy paintbrush enjoy a summer afternoon at over 13,000 feet, a testament to the hardiness of these flowers. Dominating the skyline, as it so often does in the San Juans, is Uncompahgre Peak, 14,309 feet.

MOUNT SNEFFELS
The rising winter sun highlights jewel-like facets on the northeastern
ridges of the Sneffels Range. Most climbers use picturesque Yankee
Boy Basin, behind this ridge, to attain its summit.

UNCOMPAHGRE PEAK

A fresh overnight snowfall coupled with the just rising sun paints a soft glow on the east face of Uncompahgre Peak. The climbing route largely follows the left skyline ridge and, except for the cliff zone near the top, its quite easy.

REDCLOUD PEAK • SUNSHINE PEAK

The setting sun dances through the thin clouds in a show of Mother Nature's painting skills. Redcloud Peak, 14,034 feet, and Sunshine Peak, 14,001 feet, represent large piles of steep gravel to most climbers. The status of a day's weather is often the most memorable part of climbing these twin summits.

HANDIES PEAK

Another gorgeous, albeit subtle, San Juan sunset. Here Handies is reflected in a large, grassy pond near Cinnamon Pass. Handies Peak, 14,048 feet, is easily climbed via either American Basin or Grizzly Gulch.

MOUNT EOLUS

A mountain goat nanny and her kid cruise across the "Sidewalk in the Sky" to check out the visitors invading their high domain. Diente and I had just descended from the summit of Eolus when the goats appeared on the ridge. Mount Eolus, 14,083 feet, is the highest peak in the 492,418 acre Weminuche Wilderness, Colorado's largest.

WETTERHORN PEAK

Perhaps the most common critter a climber will encounter, the yellow-bellied marmot can be seen everywhere in Colorado's mountains. Their sharp, shrill whistle accounts for another of their names, whistle pig. This marmot watches from a rock outcropping below Wetterhorn Peak, 14,015 feet.

MOUNT EOLUS

It's late June and the twin lakes of upper Chicago Basin are still frozen.
The sunlit summits of Mount Eolus, 14,083 feet and North Eolus,
14,039 feet, contrast with the shadowed Pigeon Peak, 13,972 feet.
Surprisingly, Pigeon is the most dramatic of the Needle Mountains, this
owing to its loner status to the west, and its 5,000-foot relief above
the Animas River.

SUNLIGHT PEAK • WINDOM PEAK

Across the twin lakes from Eolus and rising to an almost identical height are Sunlight Peak, 14,059 feet and Windom Peak, 14,082 feet. All three are considered difficult climbs, each with a unique set of problems. Climbers can be thankful that Sunlight is higher than Sunlight Spire, a thin rock column, just under 14,000 feet on the Sunlight—Windom connecting ridge.

MOUNT WILSON • WILSON PEAK

A San Miguel panorama that starts at Lizard Head and sweeps to Wilson Peak, with a herd of two dozen elk in the clearing between the foreground trees. The mountain panorama consists of Lizard Head, 13,113 feet; Mount Wilson, 14,246 feet; Gladstone Peak, 13,913 feet; Sunshine Mountain, 12,930 feet; and Wilson Peak, 14,017 feet.

WILSON PEAK

On the same high point where the Silver Pick rock bunkhouse sits, this group of magenta paintbrush add foreground interest to the west side of Wilson Peak. The far right saddle is Navajo Pass, part of the circle route used to access the final pitch on the east side of Wilson Peak.

Capitol Peak

This thin piece of rock is actually more exposed that it looks, it juts out over the steepest section of the summit of Capitol. Look at the cover photo to get a sense of the "get-off" from this spot. Why Diente had to go out there is beyond me. Perhaps he wanted a better view of Capitol Lake, over 2000 feet below.

El Diente Peak

Occasionally, my photo assistant would nonchalantly lay down in the foreground. On most of these events I would gently shoo him away. Fortunately, on this occasion, I fired the shutter. If you have wondered what Diente's name means and thought there might be a connection to El Diente Peak, you're right. Both are Spanish for tooth and both were well named. El Diente Peak, 14,159 feet, has a distinct tooth profile opposite this Navajo Basin perspective.

59

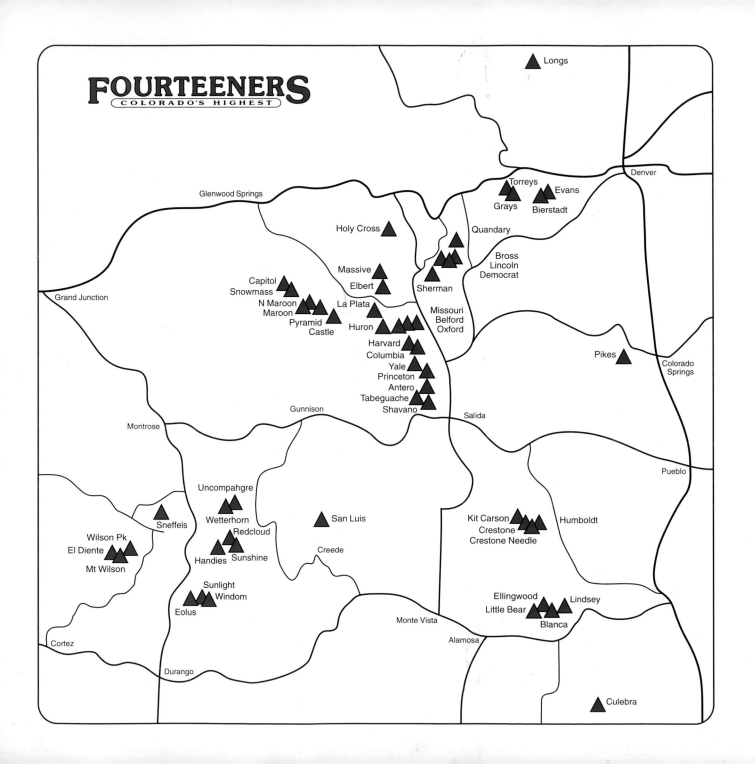

FOURTEENERS
COLORADO'S HIGHEST

Longs

Glenwood Springs

Torreys
Evans
Grays
Bierstadt

Denver

Holy Cross

Quandary

Bross
Lincoln
Democrat

Massive
Elbert
Sherman

Grand Junction

Capitol
Snowmass
N Maroon
Maroon
Pyramid
Castle

La Plata

Huron

Missouri
Belford
Oxford

Harvard
Columbia
Yale
Princeton
Antero
Tabeguache
Shavano

Pikes

Colorado
Springs

Gunnison

Salida

Montrose

Pueblo

Uncompahgre

San Luis

Kit Carson
Crestone
Crestone Needle

Humboldt

Sneffels

Wetterhorn
Redcloud

Wilson Pk
El Diente
Mt Wilson

Handies
Sunshine

Creede

Sunlight
Windom
Eolus

Monte Vista

Ellingwood
Little Bear
Blanca

Lindsey

Alamosa

Cortez

Durango

Culebra